And God Was There

AND GOD
WAS
THERE

By CHAPLAIN EBEN. COBB BRINK

75

THE WESTMINSTER PRESS · PHILADELPHIA

This book
is dedicated to my wife, Naomi, who urged its writing
that others might share these experiences which first
we shared together in letters over the seas

Foreword

THIS LITTLE BOOK has been written overseas during spare moments — if a chaplain's time can ever have spare moments — with no thought of greatness, nor attempt at literary perfection. Its stories are true, changed only as necessary to avoid the identity of personalities. Some of its incidents appeared first in *Today*, the monthly devotional booklet of the Presbyterian Church, and are retold herein because they belong rightly to this more complete story. It is written to share with others the discovery of a deeper understanding of the presence of God in a man's life. If it eases the loneliness of heavy hearts or encourages those who face serious problems, if it brings nearer to the reader the abiding presence of our Heavenly Father, it has justified its writing and the sharing of the experiences upon which it is based.

THE AUTHOR

Yesterday

I

THIS IS A STORY of men. It is the story of men who have found God — not any one man, but many men — men who have found God in unorthodox ways, in places and in experiences you and I should never have looked for him. This is a story of a chaplain too — of a chaplain who also found God, because you cannot help men to discover God without finding him anew yourself. It is a personal story — for only in a personal way can such a story be told — but it is personal only that all who read it may discover the message it is intended to bring.

The story begins in a great military training camp. Some might think it began when a Christian minister left his parish to enter the service as a chaplain. Others might feel it began much farther back — when a boy was trained by Christian parents in the way of religion, when he first learned to know *of* God, when he became a minister of the Church of Christ. But sometimes men *learn* that which they *thought they knew* before. And so this story begins in a great military camp.

Perhaps it began that day just before we sailed from home when a soldier came into the chaplain's office. His dreams were wrecked. He had wanted to go through school, to prepare himself to be a doctor. But he had been drafted, his military training was now completed, and he was being sent abroad, a gunner in a medium tank, trained now to destroy life, not to save it. A sense of futility and despair was in his soul. " I could do so much more as an individual if I could have gone on to become a doctor than I ever can as a gunner lost in massed mechanical attack. Where is God, who you, Chaplain, say is interested in an individual man? "

The chaplain, of course, had an answer for him — for men expect the chaplain to be able to tell them where God is to be found. Any chaplain, any minister, any Christian, could tell a man where God was to be found! The answer was easy — or so it seemed at that time!

Long months later the chaplain buried this same young lad beside his comrades on a battle-scarred, barren hillside many thousand miles from his home and loved ones. That night a number of men owed their lives to the valiant fight those tankers had fought. But some had had to die that day that the others might live. " I could do so much more if — . . . Where is God? " His words came hauntingly back to the chaplain — to the man of God to whom the soldier had come for an answer. And the chaplain found himself wondering what answer he had given back there in the placid security of the homeland, when battle

14

seemed so far away and we took God's presence in our midst so for granted. If only the chaplain had known then how to tell what he knew now about God's presence!

And so the story begins back in one of the great camps where we were training men to fight — and to know God. Not that every man learns to know God by entering the Army. Tragically that is far from true. The moral and spiritual breakup of lives in the Army is all too sad a story, for some there are who cannot stand the strain. This is, therefore, not the story of all men, but the story of many men, told that perhaps it might help others to learn anew the meaning of faith, to understand and be able to answer the question, " Where is God? " — answering by the experiences of some who have learned that God is wherever men will let him be, who have heard him say again, " Lo, I am with you alway, even unto the end."

II

King David may never have sailed through dangerous waters, but those who have journeyed in transoceanic convoy can understand the psalmist when he said, "I laid me down and slept; I awaked; for the Lord sustained me." It is a rude awakening for a man to find himself out on the sea, with untold dangers lurking around him, and to realize that the devices of man-made safety may all too suddenly prove futile. It is a good thing for a man to be brought face to face with himself, and to know that his only safety is in the help of the Lord. Many a man has come through that experience admitting — perhaps only in the quiet of his own mind — " I cried unto the Lord . . . , and he heard me."

Up, up, up they trudge — form after form — taking shape as men emerge at the top of the gangplanks rising from the ferries to the great gaping doorways of the huge ocean liner that looms like some great ghost out of the misty night. Man after man, endlessly, burdened down with the weight of equipment — guns slung over shoulders, barracks bags half dragged, half carried — shrouded in the dim light, strange, bewildered lads! Down, down into the bowels of the great ship they go, each to find the narrow bunk that is to be his home during the voyage — lonely men, despite the throngs of comrades milling all about them. There is no *bon voyage,* no laughter or song, none of the wild excitement commonly pictured as the way men leave home to sail forth to war. In the still watches of the night a troopship is loaded.

The transport sails out of the harbor with its precious cargo. Thousands of men fill every space, bunks rising tier upon tier. Wistful eyes grow dim as the homeland slowly vanishes below the receding horizon, but a keen glint of adventure still burns as youthful anticipation turns eager eyes toward the shores somewhere across the sea, which now rolls endlessly in its frothy billows. No one knows yet where the port of destination is to be. Necessary military secrecy adds to the tension of uncertainty.

Destroyers dart here and there, ever on the alert for the dread submarine. And now we are alone out on the open sea. The hours become nights and days, and the routine of a crowded troopship becomes a strain. Chow time with its long mess lines is followed by crowded exercise on the deck, only to be followed in turn by the long, boring passing away of time in the crowded quarters below decks. Men man the guns, ever alert for danger by air or sea. Boat drills come with alarming frequency: what to do in case of sea attack by torpedo or air attack by bombs.

The chaplain wanders among the men, laughing with them, talking with them, speaking a word to a group or an individual here or there. Nerves are on edge. Some phrase the questions: " Where are we? " " When will we get there? " " Where are we going? " And often behind the spoken question lingers the deeper thought, How safe are we? Now is the time for a word of reassurance, now is the time to remind men, facing for the first time in their lives the dreadful fear of uncertainty, that we have a God who has promised, " Lo, I am with you alway." But the words sound hollow — the ship rolls with the sea — who knows for certain that the promise is anything more than a beautiful thought?

Night follows day — and we arrive at our destination. We have crossed safely amidst the dangers. Some throw off at once the feeling of foreboding that had enveloped the ship, for after all the exuberance of youth can change its mood rapidly. But some, as they march ashore, have found a new — or a deeper — faith. Into a man's heart creeps the realization that he has found a firm ground to stand upon. He looks back at the voyage, and remembers the chaplain's text on shipboard, — a text that no longer is mere theory, but now a glad prayer of faith: " I laid me down and slept; I awakened; for the Lord sustained me." Dangers may have lurked all around — but God was there!

During the voyage the soldier had been standing at the ship's rail, a faraway look in his eyes, as the chaplain joined him silently to watch the rolling swell slip into the vanishing wake. After a while he spoke: " You know, Chaplain, I never saw the ocean before. It makes you think, doesn't it? " (This was the chaplain's cue: Turn an attentive ear, but don't talk; let the boy talk.) After a while the soldier continued, talking as much to the waves as to the one standing beside him: " Out on the plains where I come from — you know I used to raise wheat — I never thought very much about God. The church was a long way from us, and we didn't have a chance to go very often. I guess I never had religion. I used to say my prayers as a kid, but that's a long ways off now." The endless sea broke wave after wave as the boat plowed on, and together the two gazed into the deep green water. The boy lighted a cigarette. Silently he smoked, puff after puff, then turned from looking at the waves to speak directly to the chaplain:

"You know, the first night out I had a feeling I ought to say my prayers. It was funny, but the only prayer I could think of saying was the one I learned as a kid, 'Now I lay me down to sleep.' It didn't seem to help much. So I tried the Lord's Prayer — and it didn't work. I guess I finally fell asleep." He had turned back to the rail. "It's funny, but all the next day I kept thinking about it. That's when you came by and gave us those Testaments. I guess we didn't pay much attention to them. But yesterday after boat drill I got to looking at mine. I've marked the first verses I read in it — just where it opened itself as I started to look through it."

He turned his back to the wind as he took the Testament out of his pocket to read the passage: "There are not found that returned to give glory to God, save this stranger. And he said unto him, Arise, go thy way: thy faith hath made thee whole."

With a sparkle in his eye he faced the chaplain. "Chaplain — that was me! I had never said thank you to God for anything. Last night I was still thinking about it when I got in the bunk. I didn't know how to tell God — but I felt I wanted to tell him something. And as I was trying to tell him, I sort of felt he was right there near me. I know he was there."

Long months later the chaplain visited the boy in a field hospital. Proudly his Purple Heart was pinned to his pillow. The doctors said he would recover from his wounds, but not until after a long convalescence back home. " They tell me I'm lucky, Chaplain, but I tell them it wasn't luck. God gave me another chance, and I'm not going to let him down."

III

It was interesting to discover a new country — a country new to them, but older than the beloved land from which they had come. It was interesting to discover quaint customs, to drive along winding roads through a countryside that seemed to slumber as men tilled their small fields, and cut their hay with scythes. Cottages with thatched roofs never ceased to hold a romantic charm. Big-wheeled carts rolled slowly by with their loads of peat. It was all so different, and so charming, and so new to troops now training in the Emerald Isle after the great open camps they had left back home.

Maneuvers took on a new interest. There were new towns to see, with their old houses and older culture; mountains to climb, and streams to cross; ancient ruins to visit. Narrow roads wound through a countryside startled by the roar of engines and the heavy rumble of tanks and scout cars. Jeeps rushed here and there, and the country folk gazed with never-dying interest at the Yankees who had come to finish their training in this land from which so many of their fathers had sailed to settle in America.

But the novelty of new lands wore off, and men away from home and loved ones found their hearts very lonely at times. Adjustments had to be made; letters from home were slow and irregular in arriving. Some waited anxiously for word from a sick loved one. Others worried about problems left behind. Now and then one watched eagerly for the cablegram that would say the baby had arrived — only to have to await the arrival of the slower letter to let the proud father know whether the mother had presented him with son or daughter!

Men react differently when loneliness creeps in. Some find new friendships among comrades. Others learn to share the hearthside of the people in whose land they linger. Some break under the strain, trying to ease the mind with forgetfulness, creating false companionships and seeking solace in artificiality, gambling, and drink. But many there were who for the first time in their lives found themselves so alone with their thoughts that they plumbed deep into things they had taken for granted before, — that too often they had not even taken for granted.

The military police had had many problems with him. He did not seem to care for Army discipline, decency, clean entertainment, or good companionship. A " victim of the draft," he had been unwilling to adjust himself to the routine of the Army. Then one day, while he was " doing a stretch " in the guardhouse, sad news came from home. His mother was seriously ill and had not long to live. He admitted, as he talked with the chaplain, that for months he had carried unopened the Bible that his mother had given him when first he left home. We found the Bible in his barracks bag — new and unsoiled — and together in his cell we read from it. " I used to be happy when I believed this, and I never got into trouble then," he said. Several days later he sent for the chaplain. " Please send this cable to my mother. I think it will reach her in time. Just say, ' I have found your Bible again ' — she will understand."

How different were the dusty, barren plains of Tunisia from the lush, verdant hills of Ireland, when months later the chaplain received a letter through the message center from another chaplain serving in a field hospital! " You will be glad to know that Sergeant Blank is recovering nicely from his wounds. He has requested me to write you, asking you to send him his Bible. I have given him a Testament, but he wants his own Bible. He says you will find it in his barracks bag."

We found his Bible there — could this worn and thumbed Bible be the same that had been so new and unsoiled a few months ago in Ireland? The chaplain's mind turned back to a cell in a guardhouse — but he could no longer see a lonely, disillusioned private sitting there. Instead he saw a sergeant proudly leading his squad of men up a rocky hill to knock out an enemy gun position. And he remembered how after service out in a muddy field one night a corporal had knelt to be baptized. The soldier's words — what matter the rank he held this day — came back to the chaplain as he recalled that baptism: " I have learned mother was right, and I want to keep near God. Will you baptize me? "

And there were some those days who found God, not in the loneliness of their hearts, but in the very noise of the life all about them. It is a great moment in a man's life when God becomes a reality to him, when out of the silence of the night — or the noise of the day — the living voice of the Eternal is heard.

He was only a lad, like so many others, but he drove an armored scout car. He came into the chaplain's office one day to unburden his heart. We talked and we prayed together, but he could not find what he was seeking, and he went away still burdened. Then one day when the platoon had come in from a practice run, he came across the field to the chaplain. " Everything is going to be all right," he said quietly, but with a new smile on his face. " It's queer, Chaplain, but as I sat there behind the wheel during gunnery practice, I felt like praying. And in spite of all the noise, God heard me this time. I know, because I felt I could hear him answer me."

In spite of all the noise, God heard! For God was there — there in a strange land, among lonely boys training for war — there for anyone to find who would but reach out and grasp his hand. " I know, because I felt I could hear him answer me."

The months in Ireland had not only afforded the needed time for military training but had given men the opportunity to make personal adjustments to a life far from home. Tragic as those adjustments were to some, there were others who in their loneliness found new strength. Now the time had come for the final stage of training preparatory to the invasion, and the unit left the Emerald Isle that had been its camp and home. New experiences came as the men moved to England and shared for a time the life of a people on whose very doorsteps the hell of war had descended again and again.

In Ireland the Americans had learned the fortitude and uncomplaining spirit of a people rationed as the folks back home would never know rationing. In Ireland there had been signs of bombings, of families busy with the work of the home front. But it was in the heart of England that we were to discover the real courage of the home front. The British radio late in 1942 announced that one out of every five houses in England and Wales had suffered some degree of damage from the bombings since the beginning of the war. One wondered as he visited London and Coventry, as he journeyed here and there, how a people could have withstood so courageously the terror of the night. One marveled that the blackout which nightly descended upon the nation was only a physical blackout: one would not have been surprised had there been a dimming of the spirits of the people. Yet the men from America were to learn that the people who now opened their towns and homes to them were

24

still hopeful and encouraged. A new understanding of man's fortitude and faith was to be brought home to them.

It was in England that the men saw the motion picture *Mrs. Miniver,* with its soul-stirring story of today's quiet faith and heroism. Only those who have lived among people like the Minivers, who have seen their blitzed homes and churches and caught their unflinching courage, can fully appreciate the scene where the little congregation gathers to hear the minister read again: " He that dwelleth in the secret place of the most High shall abide under the shadow of the Almighty. I will say of the Lord, He is my refuge and my fortress: my God; in him will I trust. . . . Thou shalt not be afraid for the terror by night; nor for the arrow that flieth by day; . . . nor for the destruction that wasteth at noonday. . . . He shall give his angels charge over thee, to keep thee in all thy ways. . . . He shall call upon me, and I will answer him: I will be with him in trouble."

We do not usually associate a popular movie with orthodox methods of teaching a man the presence of God. Perhaps it was the emotional strain of men preparing for some great undertaking looming before them, perhaps it was the environment in which they were living — explain it as you will. The chaplain admits he was a bit surprised when a soldier came into the office the next morning, carrying his Testament in his hand. " Chaplain, the fellows in our Nissen hut last night were trying to find that passage the minister read in the picture. Will you show me where it is? "

The chaplain took from his kit another edition of the Testament, this one containing also The Psalms, which the boy's edition did not include. Together soldier and chaplain read over the passage, and for a while talked of the presence of God. As he rose to go, the lad asked, " May I keep this copy, — and could I have five more for the boys in my hut? " Before the day was over the supply of New Testaments with The Psalms included had been nearly exhausted. It was only a popular movie — but who can tell where men will find God?

IV

Surrounded by the ruins of the great blitz of London stands St. Paul's Cathedral. Complete devastation bespeaks the horror that reigned through countless bombings. Nothing stands for blocks around — nothing except St. Paul's Cathedral, blackened now by the smoke of incendiary bombs, and torn by the two bombs which hit it, but still practically unscathed! One cannot observe it without feeling that here is a parable in enduring stone. St. Paul's: the great heart of London, the center of a people's faith, majestic still amidst the ruins! But within its great, quiet sanctuary one forgets the ruins outside. True, there is a bomb hole through the side roof, and man stands awed before the great altar, where a second bomb fell. But the altar still stands, its cross " towering o'er the wrecks of time." Men and women still gather to worship before it within these stately, hallowed walls. As one leaves this quiet atmosphere and walks out to the scene of destruction, one takes new courage. Here is living proof of the Master's promise! " I will build my church; and the gates of hell shall not prevail against it."

It was naturally in the great, old churches of England that men came closer to God. At no time in the history of the battalion had church attendance been greater than it was during those weeks in Britain. Men who knew that terrific things lay not many weeks ahead thought more seriously of God and their need of him. And new experiences awaited them as they turned to the church.

It was a new experience for many to see their chaplain standing in the high pulpit of a sanctuary so kindly offered to the use of the Americans by a local congregation — a congregation which a few months before would have been shocked at the thought of a minister from another denomination preaching in their pulpit. Strange things the war has done! Perhaps that patched-up wall, where a stray bomb had damaged the building, explained the change. Perhaps the people gathered to worship — from all churches, from different nations, from all walks in life, many in uniform — felt what the Church of Christ must learn: that the mere building of one's creedal altars is not

27

enough; that religion is not a dogma to be believed, nor a rite to be performed, but a life to be lived in the Master's way. Surely the lesson that all men are brothers must begin in our churches. How else can our Christianity unite nations and establish peace upon the earth? Surely there were those who week after week gathered in churches in this distant land, finding new strength in giving themselves to the one great task of a united Christendom arrayed against the forces of evil.

Nor was it alone through the formal services in the church that men found again the truth of our religion. You have sat in your church and felt the beauty and the warmth of the stained glass windows as the daylight streamed through them. But have you thought of the many today, in lands where bombings are frequent, who enter their churches to see no beauty of the windows, because windows have been boarded up to prevent damage and to allow no light to shine out into the night? Strange, this feeling a person has in a sanctuary where the colorful beauty of symbolism has been made dark and uninspiring! Strange too the deepening sense of dependency upon God that envelops a man as he worships in the Father's house made void of its beauty because of the hatred of mankind! And then, as he leaves, he realizes that the symbolism has not been destroyed, but, rather, has taken on a new and deeper hue: Man's sin has darkened temporarily the light of the Church, has covered its beauty as with a pall, but the beauty is still there, ready to shine forth into the blackout, dispelling its gloom, whenever man will remove the barriers that prevent God's beauty from shining through.

But it was not only in great churches that men found God. Sometimes it was in simple, quiet spots. The idea grew out of young people's summer conferences held back home before the strain of war. Would it work in the rough, hard life of the Army? With a feeling of hesitancy, the chaplain found a spot for " The Upper Room," and fitted it with simple lights and an open Bible placed on the table before a small cross. In one garrison it had been the loft of an empty barn; in another it was a corner of the chaplain's tent; under more ideal conditions it was the private chapel of an old castle. But wherever it was, it became a place where a man could sit alone for a while and meditate. Men have gone there, unobtrusively and often bashfully. Men have come from there, quietly returning to their tasks. Who can tell what their thoughts have been? Who can know the strength they have found to face the trying turmoil that is all about them? Some have shared their feelings with the chaplain. Always it is the same: " It does a man good to get alone and think about God."

The blitz had destroyed the church in that little city of old England. It must have been a grand and beautiful building: the pile of debris that remained bore mute testimony to that fact. But after the planes had gone, nothing remained except a solitary wall. " Another church gone " — that was one's first impression, until one saw the bulletin board raised near the ruins. In bold letters its message stood out for the passer-by to read: " This congregation is still worshiping God. Services will be held regularly in the garage across the street." And one wondered, as one looked in at the grease-stained floor of that old garage, now filled with rough wooden benches, if God was ever worshiped in a grander cathedral. Out of the tragedy, personal and communal, of the raid's horrors, that bulletin board carries its challenge that one cannot forget: " This congregation is still worshiping God." And somehow, as one walked away, one felt that the statement was true. God dwells not in temples made with hands. He dwells, rather, wherever a man finds him — and, finding him, shares his presence with another man.

V

And then the long-awaited orders came. The days of training were completed. Great, mysterious, secret moves were under way. Somewhere an invasion was about to be launched. Men and vehicles, stores and supplies, were loaded on many boats. Ours was not to be the task of the first invasion landing. Ours was the task of following up that invasion and then of joining the first forces to drive the enemy out of a land that totalitarian tyranny had seized in its bid for world domination.

Through storm-tossed seas a great convoy sailed —

through mighty Gibraltar, and into the quiet of the Mediterranean. Of the events of that trip historians will long years later still be writing. It was filled with days of strain and uncertainty. But the chaplain noticed that men who in the first ocean voyage months before had so clearly shown their nervousness, now faced the greater dangers of this trip with calm expectancy. Could it be that during the months of training a new assurance had come into their lives? Further events would tell.

The ships carrying the task force sailed on. Planes from the convoying carriers dropped their bombs off in the distance, telling all too plainly the dangers that lurked under the placid waters. Destroyers discharged their depth bombs. Men waited apprehensively, but somehow everyone knew that when the dread torpedo hit there would be no excitement. Men were ready and knew just what they were to do. As the chaplain went from deck to deck, speaking now a word of encouragement, giving here a Testament, offering there a moment's prayer, he knew that among his men there were many who had found that God was with them — and would be with them until the attending destroyers brought the crippled ship safely to shore.

And so we came to Africa.

Strange forebodings took possession of men's minds. One felt the tension all about. Only a few days before, this had been an alien land. Now some who had fought against the Americans' landing were our allies in the common cause of ridding this land of the usurping enemy. Some still secretly gave allegiance to the foe. Dangers real and imagined lurked on every side. Men who had lived in the theory of blackout now discovered it was no longer theory. Guards walking their posts at night listened warily to disturbing sounds. But the stars shone brightly — as they so often shine through the blackout.

At least one thing has come to man as a blessing out of the depressing blackout through which he lives in the long hours of the night: he has learned to see the stars, and finds that the darker the night, the brighter is their message of eternal assurance — of a God who sets the stars in their course and who holds the universe in his hand. To the lonely, discouraged man, fearful of the dread things about him, the stars twinkle a cheery encouragement: " God's in his heaven," and all will yet be " right with the world."

And so they shone that Christmas Eve as lonely men in a strange land stood alerted. The Christmas carol service had been interrupted as the news had flashed from headquarters to headquarters: " Alert the men. Stand ready for whatever trouble may come. Darlan has been assassinated! " Men already keyed to the point of tension became alert, and waited — for what? And the stars shone down, reflected from myriad pools where deep mud still held the rains that had fallen so often during the past days. Long years before, these same stars had looked down upon a troubled world on that first Christmas Eve. Would that men tonight might hear the angels sing, " On earth peace, good will toward men "! But now as the stars shone down, men dared not raise their voices even in the songs of carols — lest as they stood alert they might not catch the sound of some lurking foe. So, slowly, the long night passed, and it was Christmas Day!

There are countless men who will never forget that Christmas — their first Christmas away from home. Other men will spend other Christmas Days away from home — in camps, on battlefields, out on the sea, in the air, — and each will best remember his own first Christmas in a strange land. For those particular ones of whom this story is written, it was a lonely Christmas. Mud lay everywhere, ankle-deep, reminding men of the rainy season now nearing its end. Mails had been seriously delayed because of the recent invasion — it was to be months yet before the long-anticipated Christmas packages from home finally got through — and lonely men dreamed of home, and went about the day's tasks. It was hard to follow the Wise Men that day.

It was evening before the spirit of Christmas really came into the camp. The sudden fear of the last night's alert had grown less during the day as it had become evident that the assassination would have no inflammatory effects upon the populace of the country. As the tension wore off, voices lifted in song, and the Christmas carols, so rudely interrupted the eve before, rang out through the darkness. And the stars shone down as they had shone down so many years ago, and some who listened heard, not the chaplain's voice, but an angel voice: " Unto you is born . . . a Saviour."

It was only an impromptu service, held with those who had come together informally to sit on ammunition boxes, ration cases — on anything that offered a seat above the deep mud — and to sing together the songs of Christmas. As the chaplain stopped speaking, men sat in that silence which speaks so eloquently of thoughts too deep for words. The stars shone down through the blackout — had ever they shone so brightly before? One by one, in groups of twos and threes, the men wandered back to their pup tents on Christmas night.

Two months later in Tunisia, when long overdue Christmas packages had finally caught up with men resting for a while from battle, a soldier shared a letter with the chaplain — a letter that had come with a present from home. "This Bible, son, is the one your father carried through the First World War," the letter said. "We want you to read a passage in it each day, beginning this first Christmas Day that you are away from home. Will you do this for your father and mother?" The chaplain handed the letter back to the soldier. "Why don't you write and tell them you will do as they ask?" There was a peculiar joy on his face as the soldier answered: "That's just it, Chaplain, I've already done so. I did it back there in Algeria the day after Christmas. You know, after we sang those carols, I sat outside of my tent for a long time watching the stars. Then I got out the Testament you had given me and read the Christmas story — and the next morning I wrote home and told the folks I had promised God I would keep on reading his Word — and

34

here this Bible was waiting to be delivered all that time." And so the stars had shone down that Christmas Eve as lonely men stood alerted in a strange land.

The first few weeks in Africa have passed. The rains have ended, and we have moved out of the mud which covered men and vehicles in Algeria to the dusty, sunbaked borders of Tunisia — and to battle! Some who made the long march had already learned that God was with them, while others were yet to have that experience which would enable them to say, " And God was there."

Today

I

"TURN THEM OVER!" Through the darkness just before daybreak, the order is repeated from scout car to jeep, from tank to half-track, from man to man. The pregnant silence comes alive with the noise of armored vehicles poised ready for the attack. "Turn them over!" The familiar command to move, heard so often in maneuvers, now orders the armored force into its first battle. So this is what we have been waiting and training for!

Vehicle after vehicle slides noisily through the blackout, moving up to that dread something that lies waiting ahead. Men sit in their places, tense with an emotion they had never felt before — would often feel again. Eyes peer out into the darkness, trying in vain to see — wishing it were light, yet fearing the coming of dawn. A machine gun cracks out somewhere — rat! tat! tat! — the too nervous trigger finger of a tense gunner, that is all.

Radio operators nervously touch the dials — fearing that the all-important link of communication entrusted to them might not work clearly. What was that flare over yonder? Men gaze into the sky. Faint traces of the dawn begin to dim the stars, but eyes are not looking at stars. Fantastic shadows seem to be even in the heavens — no, it is not light enough yet for the dread dive bomber to come hurtling out of the rising sun to pay its morning visit. Slowly, cautiously, the roaring machines move out toward the place where the foe is waiting. Do the enemy know, or shall we be able to surprise them?

More than the engines of military machines were turning over as the dawn broke that morning. A few hours earlier, the orders had been given for this first day in battle. Maps had been studied in the crowded command tent. Each platoon leader had been given the specific instructions for his section. All was ready — ready in the cold, precise manner of a military machine. Just before dawn the order would come, " Turn them over! " But before then catch a few minutes of sleep! Rest your bodies, relax the tense muscles! But who could relax when minds were turning over so many thoughts, when men all about were silently apprehensive, when a thousand and one moments crowded into the present instant? Relax! What are the folks back home doing? Rest! What is going to happen tomorrow? Relax!

> " Now I lay me down to sleep,
> I pray Thee, Lord, my soul to keep.
> If I should die . . .
> I pray Thee, Lord, my soul to take."

The grown man knelt beside his bedding roll there on the ground. (Other nights he had said his prayers — for he was one who prayed each night — after he had crawled under the blankets. But somehow, to-night, it seemed a little more fitting to kneel as he used to kneel beside the real bed at home.) "Now I lay me down . . ." (But why *this* prayer? I haven't said this prayer since I was a child! There are other things to pray for tonight.) "Dear God, be with my loved ones — be with me — now I lay me down — to sleep." Rest! Relax! Even tense nerves and disturbed minds fell into slumber for the few remaining hours of night. Then the zero hour!

"Turn them over!" Covered by the thick darkness that hangs heavy just before the dawn breaks, vehicles and men respond. Thank God for the protection of the blackout! No! rather let the light come — O God, where art thou? What's going to happen?

Out over the plain they spread, crawling slowly forward, now around a wadi, now cautiously approaching a barren hill. Slowly the advance vehicles inch their way to the crest of the hill, delaying as long as possible the inevitable silhouette that may first draw enemy fire.

Suddenly out of the sun they come — roaring down in their hellish dive. Guns blaze, bullets stream from planes as they mercilessly strafe vehicles and men who have flattened themselves on the ground. Who will ever know the thoughts or the prayers of a man when

41

first he is the target of a strafing attack? Can those marks there on the ground just an arm's length away really be the pattern of the bullets sprayed by the fast-passing plane? What about the other men? Mustn't stay here! Must get going!

Down! Here they come again — zooming back for another attack. O God! How many times are they going to try for us? That truck there! It's hit! It's burning! Get the gunner off — he's shot!

Men who a moment before lay prone upon the ground, trying as if by the power of their fear alone to sink into the solid earth, away from the bullets, suddenly find their feet. Easy! He's badly hurt. Here's the stretcher. Move away from the truck — it's loaded with demolition kits and may blow up. Easy! Men who have never seen so much blood before kneel beside the stretcher to give help to the young doctor who, white-faced and tense, is trying calmly to go about this new task that is his. Here they come again! But this time the little group only duck their heads — there's a job to be done. And as the planes roar past, they scarcely look up.

The chaplain too kneels beside the stretcher. He speaks into the ear of the wounded man the words of faith — words which he had always known would be the words to speak at such a time. A jeep drives up, bringing two more wounded men. Stretchers are placed for them on the ground. The doctor looks hurriedly at their injuries and turns back to the first, more serious case. The chaplain speaks to each of them — carefully chosen words — just the right words at such a time! Finally the wounds are dressed — the ambulance has moved off to the field hospital. Medical men and chaplain move forward to rejoin the others.

And now a halt comes. The rough, barren hills are just ahead, and in and behind those hills are the enemy strongholds. There is a final breathing space — a rest — before the battalion moves into actual battle. The tenseness is terrific. Every man has his own thoughts — too deep and sacred and personal to probe. The chaplain's mind is disturbed. Those men who were sent back to the hospital — the words he spoke to them — how hollow they sounded as he repeated them — the prayer he had whispered in their ears — had they felt his own doubt in its phrases? Doubt? Surely the chaplain could have no doubt, no fear; he was a man of faith. But he had feared, he had doubted, as he lay hugging the earth. Where was his faith? How could even he believe that God could be in the midst of such terror and horror?

" Mount up, turn them over! " The order sounded from vehicle to vehicle. And then it happened — a dust-covered private stopped beside the chaplain's car. He had been with the outfit all the past months, but somehow the chaplain did not then recall his name. His grimy face shone with a cheery smile. " Chaplain, I just wanted you to know I was praying that that truck would not blow up while you and the doctor were working back there awhile ago."

Praying that the truck would not blow up while you

43

were there! Why, that's right — the explosion had come with terrific force *after* the ambulance and the group had left! Who could say that God had not heard that prayer? And if he heard it, he must have been there! Slowly the chaplain himself began to understand. Back there he had seen only the horror, had felt only the terror of diving, strafing aircraft, the thick, oozing lifeblood of a wounded man. The words of eternal truth he had spoken had been false in his own ears because he had doubted God's presence. But someone else had believed, and in his belief had prayed to the God who he knew was near enough to hear even over the whine of propellers and the roar of flames — had prayed not for himself but for someone else!

The chaplain had learned his lesson. Surely God was in that place and he knew it not! Before a man can share with others the knowledge of the presence of God, he must know that presence himself. Only thus can the eternal words he would speak carry conviction to others.

II

Somehow that long first day of battle came to an end. There would be other days — many other days. Those minutes that were hours long would be longer still in the days that would follow. Other stretchers would be laid on the ground, and other ambulances would go back and forth. Other crosses on the hillsides of other places would silently mark the tragedy and

44

cost of man's sacrifice. But somehow that first long day of battle came to an end. Tired men dug their slit-trenches before weary bodies could take their rest. Guards, wakeful in spite of their need of sleep, kept careful watch until they were relieved. Strange shadows rose in the blackout from vehicles ready for the next move before dawn should break on another day.

The staff came out of the command tent, carefully moving through the double flaps to prevent any ray of light from showing out into the darkness, lest some hostile eye might see it. Inside the tent, maps had been spread, plans had been discussed, orders had been given; a military machine was carefully molding the pattern for another day's battle, coldly calculating every detail. Outside, a battalion wearily slept, grotesque figures in their blankets, veiled by the darkness of the blackout.

Two or three of the staff stood silently outside the tent before going to their own bedrolls. They whispered together, in that strange, hushed voice which the blackout seemed to impel. One of them said to his fellow officers: "The stars seem very close to earth tonight. It doesn't seem that we were killing men here a few hours ago. Makes you feel like God was here!"

The chaplain walked over to his jeep, cautiously feeling his way through the darkness. A sentry spoke, his voice betraying the emotion of one who alone in the darkness feared even the sound of his own voice: "Halt! — advance and be recognized."

A lonely boy and a chaplain lingered to whisper together for a few minutes. Which wadi did your platoon cross today? Which hill seemed to you to have the most enemy hiding in it? What's going to happen tomorrow? Yes, the stars are bright tonight. Yes, it all makes a fellow think — but, no, he doesn't put much stock in religion or prayer. If a shell's got your number on it, that's all there is to it; if it hasn't, that's your luck. No, he doesn't care to share a word of prayer before the chaplain goes on.

Tomorrow night he will be on guard again. The chaplain will look him up at his post and talk further with him. Tomorrow night — but will he? Before tomorrow night there will be more fighting. Go back and speak to him again tonight. Ask him about home, get him talking about his loved ones. Soften his heart. Leave some memory working in his mind, some thought to dwell upon there under the stars as he stands guard over his sleeping comrades. Let him know he is not alone, that God is there, waiting in the shadows, to share the darkness with him. Go back to him. Even though you are tired, chaplain, go back to him.

Other days and nights passed, and the records one day carried the brief notice that he was missing in action. Months later, when word had been received that he was a prisoner of war, a letter came to the chaplain from the boy's mother:

" Thank you so much for the word you sent us about our son. I have just received a letter from him, the first in four months. He is well and seems to be happy.

He wants to be remembered to all the boys in the battalion and says to ask you to tell them that he prays for them every night as he looks at the stars. He says to tell you that they are the same stars you and he watched one night when you came back to tell him God was standing guard beside him."

Days and nights lengthened into weeks, and weeks became months — and battle followed battle. There were few periods of rest for the reconnaissance battalion, for always the enemy must be watched, its positions and movements constantly observed and reported. In the fast shifting scenes of armored warfare, the battalion covered great sectors of a front that reached into many parts of Tunisia. And always there were things to try men's souls: machine-gun nests to face, artillery positions to storm, mine fields to locate. But always men went bravely on, and some found strength in the knowledge that God was with them, knowing that he would never leave them nor forsake them.

The artillery barrage had begun before dawn. Only men who have been awakened by the thunder and crash of artillery roaring out of the blackness of the night can know the ominous foreboding that accompanies such a barrage. And with the dawn, the tanks had come rolling over the plain, through the passes, in a great, encircling attack. Hour after hour through that day, successive waves of tanks met the cold steel of enemy armor. And when at last another night gave brief respite to battle, many units of those which had borne the brunt of the attack were missing. That night the enemy counted many prisoners, captured in the pass that the reconnaissance company had been watching. They might have got out — that company — but an army depended upon their holding fast that day, and they held, allowing others to withdraw safely before the advancing armor of the foe.

The days that followed, before the tide of battle was to turn, were dark in the hearts and minds of those who thought of comrades left behind. It would be many long months before the slow reports from prison camps would clear through Geneva, and men would know what had happened to some of those who had stayed there in the pass. Meanwhile, a few did find their way back. Hiding by day, stealthily creeping by night, taking long chances, enduring thirst and hunger, somehow they got through the enemy lines and back to their friends.

He was a tall, heavy-set officer two weeks ago when he went with his men on their mission. Today as he sat in the chaplain's tent, there was a worn, gaunt look on his face. Flesh which only a few days before had been solid, now hung flabby on his limbs. One could tell, without hearing his story, that he had been through hell. With a faraway look in his eyes he told of how the enemy had closed in around them, and how he and his platoon had tried to get away. You saw with him the anguish of that day, and the greater anguish of that night when, trying to find a way for his men to get through, he lost contact with them. You felt with him the helplessness of a man who has lost his compass, the thirst of a man whose canteen is empty, the hunger of a man who goes for days with little to eat, and the solitude of a man alone in enemy territory. Somehow, after more than a week of hiding by day and sneaking by night, he had got through the enemy lines and safely back to friendly territory. Now, worn and tired, he sat in the chaplain's tent, telling again of his experiences as a few minutes before he had told his commanding officer.

" Chaplain, I surely was glad I believed in God. I never could have done it without him. He was all the company I had out there, and I owe him a lot. If he had not been with me, I would not be here today. I never realized before what it means to trust in God." They were not the words of a novitiate, but the confession of faith of one who was known among men as a Christian Churchman, who now had found a newer, deeper meaning to his faith, who now felt anew the presence of God.

Somewhere up ahead the enemy forces are located. Before a successful attack can be launched, the reconnaissance units must go forward to locate their positions. A " phantom battalion," the reconnaissance men must not only be able to see without being seen and to hear without being heard, but they must also find the way for others to go. From what they learn and report back to headquarters, the army makes its plans to move forward. To go out day after day and night after night, finding where the enemy strength may be, groping into strange territory, knowing not at what moment a platoon may come upon an enemy-held strong point, takes real courage. Often as he talked with the men, the chaplain discovered the desire in their hearts for the assurance of God, for some proof of the certainty of his reality, of his presence. A word of encouragement, a thought to cherish, a verse of Scripture to echo in their minds, a whispered prayer — something to hold to as they went forth to reconnoiter — and men faced more easily the unknown before them.

Of all the dread creations of war, the land mine and booby traps are among the most feared — nefarious traps, insidiously set to explode when the unsuspecting person moves over them. The fear of the mine field is natural to every man, however brave. Danger lurks around every turn, in every wadi — wherever the enemy has had time to set his mine. Engineers, trained in the removing of mine fields, have well earned the admiration of their fellow soldiers for their valiant work in clearing the way for troops to move. To reconnaissance men falls the task of locating the mined areas. A man is very much alone when he is probing for land mines, pushing the point of his bayonet into the earth, feeling for the metallic ring that will tell of the hidden danger — alone though he may be flanked by comrades also probing, step by step, until the dangers be removed and the way be cleared for others to pass.

"I do not dare to think of the danger," said one as he talked of the job. "All I know is that I must go on, slowly, carefully — that I must not be hurried." And as we talked, another said, "That's when I say my prayers, as I hit the mine field."

The conversation was lighthearted enough, with that studied lightheartedness that denotes men covering a worried seriousness. "What do you pray about then?" asked a third in the group. The answer was trite, as one would expect, "That God will keep me safe."

Trite, commonplace phrases, lightly spoken. How often men have prayed that God would keep them safe! Then after a moment the first man spoke again: "I never thought of it before, but if I were going to pray about it, I don't think I could ask God to keep me safe. Rather, I think I would have to ask him to help me to find the mines and then help me to remove them."

No one that night had expected this to be a discussion of the theology of prayer; no one had expected it to be a forum of religion. But there in the wheat-fields on the hillside, the chaplain sat with a group of men. They talked of mines and of prayer. They spoke of men and of God. And before they retired to rest they shared an evening prayer together, and one who had

51

" never thought of it before," that night asked God to stay with him and help him. Weeks later, when the battles in Africa were over and mine fields had been left far behind, the same soldier knelt to be baptized before partaking of the Communion. " I want to belong to God," he humbly told the chaplain as he made his confession of faith, " because I know I need his help now even as I needed it up there."

A man is very much alone when he is probing for land mines, except when God is with him. And God was there.

III

" The Lord is my shepherd; I shall not want. . . . In my Father's house are many mansions. . . . And, lo, I am with you alway, even unto the end."

A small group stands beside the open grave, heedless of the shells which whine unseen overhead. One gets used to the sound of artillery shells; one feels or hears instinctively after a while which shell will pass and which is close enough to cause a man to drop to the ground.

" I am the resurrection, and the life: . . . whosoever liveth and believeth in me shall never die."

The brief service is over; the grave is carefully marked to await the day when war shall end, and the honored dead shall be taken back to sleep their long sleep in the hallowed soil of the homeland. The little group turn away — they cannot linger, for there is so much to do.

The way back to headquarters leads over an engineer's bridge. Twice on the way out the driver had to stop before crossing the bridge to await a break in the enemy artillery fire trying to bracket in on its span. Would the bridge still be there, and could we return over it? The chaplain glances at his driver's face. A grim determination marks the set of his chin. His face is white, with the whiteness that comes only to one who knows what he has to fear. His hands grasp the steering wheel with an iron grip. And now the bridge is just ahead — and now the car speeds over it! Safe! A cold perspiration breaks out on the brow of each who rides across. No one speaks for several minutes. Finally the driver turns to the chaplain, " Yes, He is still with us! "

Some might think there was an irreverence in the way the words were spoken, but in the days that had passed that expression had become a byword between them. Side by side they had seen frequent proofs of the presence of God, and it was a devout confession often expressed by the one to the other. It was an expression of a growing understanding of the presence of God, not only in the moments of personal peril, but also in the lives of others.

The battlefield offers, to those who are able to listen amidst the turmoil of conflict, a stirring study of men's souls. During engagements the opportunities of holding worship services are of course rare, if such opportunities present themselves at all. But it is during such days that the chaplain comes nearest to the hearts of men. Kneeling beside the wounded as the doctors care for them, speaking words of assurance, sharing the privilege of prayer, taking down some message for the loved ones at home — a thousand and one little intimacies reveal so often the true soul of a man.

The chaplain bent over one, lifting his head that he might quench the burning thirst from the canteen held to his lips. Others lay beside him on the ground while doctors and aid men gave them emergency treatment. " Tell the doctor to take care of the others first; I'll be all right. But I am not so sure of the others." His voice was weak, breath came in short gasps. The chaplain knew that the sergeant was badly wounded, but when he would call the doctor to care for him, a smile showed on the swollen lips. " No, Chaplain, they need him more than I do. I'm not afraid to die if God says so this time. He has never failed me before and I'm not afraid. But some of my men there are not ready to die. They need the doctor more than I do. I'll be all right. You go to them."

" Greater love hath no man than this, that a man lay down his life for his friends."

That night the corporal who took his place came to the chaplain's pup tent. " He used to talk to us about God, Chaplain, and we never paid much attention to what he said. But somehow tonight I feel he was right. I've got to take his place, but I want to know what he knew about God." Men need sleep, but the stars that looked down that night had circled far in the heavens when finally chaplain and corporal knelt together in prayer: " Lord, I believe; help thou mine unbelief."

There are times during battle when men are called upon to do things not included in the training manuals. Every officer and man carries on his belt the little first-aid packet: emergency bandage, sulphanilamide pills and powder, morphine syrets; but sometimes these are not enough. Sometimes neither doctor nor aid men are present when a need arises. Such was the case in that tank knocked out by enemy fire, when the officer tried to extricate the driver before further shell-fire should demolish it completely. But the driver's leg was hopelessly caught in the wrecked vehicle. Only an amputation could free him. Only a pocketknife in the hands of an officer was available. Later when fellow officers were complimenting him for what he had done, his reply was humble and sincere: " It had to be done, and I prayed for strength to do it. God heard me, for I couldn't have done it without him."

Thus often on the field of battle men who faced danger and trying tasks felt the Presence and Strength beyond their own. Someone has said that the biggest kind of courage is the ability to sit still in the midst of danger. To the men of reconnaissance, there were often long periods of sitting still, on a hilltop, behind a boulder, in a wadi; long periods of observation, trying to see without being seen, to hear without being heard. Men have been decorated for the steadfast gallantry with which they occupied lonely observation posts.

From such an assignment the lad came to the chaplain. Often before he had held such posts, often again it would be his lot. But this morning he wanted to talk to someone who would understand. " Chaplain, I'm not afraid. I'm not worried. But out there on OP I've been doing a lot of thinking. I've never done anything really very wrong, but still I've never done anything very good. Yet out there I got to thinking about everything. If anything should happen to me, I want you when you write to my folks to tell them that everything was all right, for I have talked with God out there while I was alone." While he was alone! No — with artillery shells flying over him, with the distant enemy in sight as he watched through his binoculars — he was not alone. God was there: he had talked with him!

Frequently the men would come to the chaplain before going into an engagement, bringing an envelope, a package, a trinket, or some other possession: " Chaplain, please hold this for me until it's over. If I don't come back, please send it home for me." And when, sometimes, the lad did not come back, the chaplain opened the envelope, as censorship required, before it could be sent home. The tender confidences contained therein cannot be betrayed. But one had a message that ought to be known. The mother to whom it was sent has told the chaplain he might share it, for this is what the lad wrote:

" I have tried in my letters not to worry you, for I have known how you must fear daily for my safety. But I want to leave one final message for you if anything should happen to me. Somehow I feel I will not come home again. It is a strange feeling, with no fear in it. It is a quiet feeling, that I want you to understand, as I think you can. Every day since you taught me to pray as a little child at your knee, I have always prayed to God. My happiest thoughts are of you and father praying at home for me as I over here am praying for you. And lately, as I have said my daily prayers, I have felt that God was nearer to me than ever before. We've had some pretty dirty jobs to do, but still God has been very close to me. In spite of what goes on around me, I still feel he is nearer every day. And tonight I feel that he is so near I can almost see him. If anything does happen, and I don't come home to you, I want you to know that I am not afraid, for I will be safe with him."

A few hours after he had written that letter, and deposited it with the chaplain for safekeeping, the lad had gone out on another reconnaissance mission. Later as we turned away from the rough cross marking another hallowed spot, one of his comrades who had come back from the mission, laid some desert flowers on the new-turned soil, and stood for a moment in final salute before the grave. Everyone there understood: those who had come back owed their safety to the comrade who had volunteered to stay that they might return. " If anything does happen, and I don't come home to you, I want you to know that I am not afraid, for I will be safe with Him."

But it was not only in the tragedy of the battlefield that one could see men finding God. Testimony has been borne by others to the discovery that " there can be no atheists in foxholes." It has been said that a soldier's two indispensable items of equipment are his rifle and his shovel. Statisticians may some day compute how far slit-trenches dug end to end would reach, or how far the total depth of foxholes would penetrate into the ground, but science will never be able to fathom the emotions of men crouched in the holes they have dug for themselves. Only a man who has heard the whine of roaring dive bombers, and the thud of exploding bombs, who has pushed deep against the bottom of his trench as though by the very pressure of his body he would make it even deeper, who has lived through the minutes that seem hours in a foxhole, can ever understand. But to those who have had the experience, there is no mystery about a man's admitting that he was praying while he lay there.

True, the emotional prayer offered when danger seems so close at hand is often forgotten when that danger has passed. But there are those who, forced to resort to prayer, have found through it the fellowship with God which they had ignored before, a fellowship that once found can never be fully forgotten. A man cannot come into the presence of the Almighty without being impressed with the beauty of that Presence, even though he turn to sordid things again.

The campaign had ended weeks before, and the division had been resting and refitting far from the scenes of battle, when the chaplain was invited to spend an evening in a tent with five men. A can of cookies from home, a box of fudge from a sweetheart — both stale and in crumbs, but tastier than cookies or fudge fresh in a tidy kitchen ever could be — a bit of cheese and coffee, and the makings of a party were complete. Conversation was easy these days — there were plenty of experiences to be hashed over and over again. The conversation shifted to religion, to God, to a Saviour, to prayer.

"That's what we asked you to come here for tonight, Chaplain. We were talking about it last night, and we admitted to each other that up there when things were hot, we had prayed, but we haven't prayed since. We decided last night we ought to keep it up, but somehow it just didn't come. So we decided to get you in tonight to show us how."

There are times when a chaplain feels very small and very humble. It was not an officer who sat there that evening and talked with enlisted men. It was not a chaplain who knelt finally with them beside their bunks. Somehow into our midst another Presence had come, and together all six in that tent heard him speak. Once again the fellowship that had lingered for but a moment with men in a Tunisian slit-trench was experienced. Such a fellowship once found can never be fully forgotten. It may come soon again, it may be long in returning. But the men in that tent that night found that when hearts are opened to receive God, he will never leave them nor forsake them. Such is the fellowship of God with man.

IV

This story would not be complete were it not to tell of formal worship services. Yet to call them formal services is a serious misnomer. The chaplain is required by Army law to conduct services regularly, to arrange so that men in his battalion (if he be a Protestant) shall have the service of Catholic or Hebrew chaplains when possible. At home, in camp or in bivouac, the responsibility is easily accomplished. But when troops have gone overseas it is often difficult, if not impossible, for men to have a chaplain of their own faith. Thus it is that a unit chaplain becomes a servant to all men, and his services lose narrow sectarianism. Even worship becomes informal, that men may feel no hesitation or strangeness in a worship whose form may differ from that which they knew before.

The very setting of services becomes an interesting commentary on how men discover the presence of God. Men no longer come to a cathedral, or to a country church, or even to an Army chapel — those were left behind long months ago. Now they come to the open hillside, or gather in a wadi or under the olive trees — wherever the chaplain's flag may be flying for this hour of divine worship. Sometimes the service must of necessity be held after dark, that the blackout may give that protection which alone allows men to gather in groups. Often, very often, the groups are small, but when the opportunity allows, full congregations will gather before the little portable altar set up by the chaplain on a box of " C " rations, on a boulder, or on the back of his car. Frequently it is not even Sunday, for days of the week have little meaning to men in combat. But as they gather, wherever or however it be, they have learned the first lesson of true worship: that men can find God even in the midst of turmoil. They have discovered that God is found, " not in temples made with hands," but wherever men humbly seek to worship him.

A few services stand out in bold relief as the picture of these months rolls by. There was that little service held during the final days of training in England, after which the chaplain, as an Army officer, was asked to censor a soldier's letter. Because the chaplain wanted to remember it, the soldier gave him permission to copy part of the letter. " I have just come back from Communion," the lad wrote to his mother. " It was held this time in the beautiful, tiny chapel that is part of this old castle where we are living. The flickering candlelights made you feel as if God was in the shadows all about you. I had the same feeling I told you about after our last Communion, the one we held out under the trees where the chaplain set up the altar on the back of his jeep. I felt God was there too. I know I do not do all I should, for I drink and swear sometimes, but as I prayed tonight I felt God was near me and near you at home. I never understood before why they called it Communion, but I understand now. I came back to my bunk knowing that whatever is ahead of us, he will stay near me if I keep near him."

Other Communion services were to follow. There are men who will never forget how near God came to them as they knelt in the deep mud of Algeria on New Year's Eve to receive the bread and the cup just before they were to move on toward Tunisia. There are veterans of Sidi Bon Zid and Kasserine Pass who knelt under the cover of the blackout to pray for their missing comrades and to thank God for their own deliverance as they again shared the fellowship of a Saviour. Time and again, in groups and individually, men would receive the Sacrament from the hands of the chaplain, and would take new courage as they remembered Him who had died for them.

The service of Holy Week will probably linger longest in the minds of some who then found God in Tunisia. The southern phase of the campaign was over. The division had reassembled. Replacement of men and vehicles was completed. On Palm Sunday the battalion would be moving northward by forced march. But tonight, Friday, the battalion was together. Palm trees growing near by gave of their branches to build an altar on the back of the chaplain's car. Natives passed down the roadway, urging on their patient, overburdened burros. Here and there ambling camels plodded across the barren fields. Somehow one forgot the machines of armored warfare that bespoiled the view and saw only the humble peasantry that reminded men of the time when Christ rode into the city on a burro. And as the rays of the setting sun stole across the heat-parched fields, the Spirit of God was very near to those who bowed in prayer before him — very near to those who came forward that night to be baptized and to confess the faith they had found when through the noise of past battles the still, small voice had come to them: " Lo, I am with you alway."

The long, hard march to the north, the few feverish days of preparation for another campaign, made it hard for any to remember that this was Holy Week. All the tense fear of past days came again into men's hearts as they faced further battle. They were still waiting, poised, ready for the orders to move forward on Good Friday. So scattered were the positions the battalion held that the chaplain found it necessary to hold several services to give all the men an opportunity to attend. He had expected good attendance, for, after all, it was Good Friday. But even the chaplain, accustomed never to expect anything definite when it came to men's attending services, was surprised at the large group that met him at each bivouac site.

This was no time to preach sermons. Here on the hillsides before him the chaplain realized he faced men even as the Master had faced men long years ago on other hillsides. They were men who had difficult tasks to do, men who had been called to leave homes and loved ones; some of them were going to die for the cause they believed in. It was no time for theories.

Now was the time to tell the old, old story, as simply as ever it had been told, as simply and as beautifully as the Master would tell it if he were there among these men.

And the Master was there. Weeks later the chaplain received a letter from a mother who had received the dread telegram: " The Secretary of War desires me to express his deep regret that your son was killed in action in defense of his country." Even in her sorrow there was peace in her heart that she wanted to share. " I thought you would like to know," the mother wrote the chaplain, " that the last letter I received from my son was written the morning after the Good Friday service. He said that he had found God in that service, and that he understood now what it meant that Christ had died for him. He closed his letter by saying he was not afraid of the coming battle, because he knew he would be safe with God whatever happened."

Between Good Friday and Easter morn the battalion waited. And then the orders came! Tonight move into position to enter " The Mousetrap " tomorrow morning — " The Mousetrap " so called because it was a plain between high ridges, and could easily prove a trap for the forces that must pass through it! Every man knew the task ahead, every man knew the enemy might spring the trap before its fortifications could be seized and its jaws prevented from closing. Did ever men face an Easter morn with more reason to doubt? Did ever a minister face a greater Easter congregation than those groups who gathered in their combat suits, sitting on their upturned helmets, there on the hillsides? " ' Go . . . , tell his disciples and Peter ' that ' he is risen.' " The glorious message of that first Easter Day was the message for today.

" Tell his disciples " — for there were disciples on those hillsides that morning, men who had always been faithful to the Master of whom they had learned in childhood and youth, men who in the weeks and months past had learned to know him, and to feel that God walked with them; " and Peter " — for there were Peters there too, men who had known their Lord but who had failed him, men who yet needed to know him and learn to take his presence into their lives: " Christ is risen — ' he goeth before you'! "

The company commander waited until the last of the men had gone back to their vehicles. " Chaplain, I don't know what's ahead — but as I saw my men kneeling there at the close of the service — I knew we cannot fail. I've always believed in God, as you know. But I prayed today that my men might know as I lead them into ' The Mousetrap ' that I'm asking God to give me guidance and to be with each one of them as he has always been with me. And if we get through, I know it will be because he has been with us who are trying to ring true."

The battalion got through " The Mousetrap " — and on through those bitter days of struggle that followed in rapid succession until the enemy surrendered, and victory had come to the men in Africa.

With the coming of victory came the rout of the enemy. Strong men, now come to the end of their might, surrendered in ever-increasing numbers. There is something tragic, even in the emotional thrill of victory, at the sight of weary, dejected men stumbling toward a refuge they have been forced unwillingly to seek. It speaks well for the spark of humanity that glows in the warrior's breast to note how soon the passion of the battle front can pass. A few hours before they had been engaged in mortal combat. Now they were face to face as men. True, they were still the foe — vanquished now, and perforce to be treated as prisoners — but they were also men. They too had their homes and loved ones, and they too were lonely and homesick for parents and wives and sweethearts.

There was little opportunity to talk with them, even when one could speak their language, for they came in such increasing numbers that it taxed the facilities to care for them. Rapidly they were sent farther back to the hastily enclosed prison camps. Now and then one stopped to ask a drink of water, to rest a wounded leg, to ease a weary body. Most of them were silent, with the silence that comes from bewilderment. But all of them were men — and the chaplain tried to let those who stopped near his car know that there were no enmities under the flag of blue with its cross of white.

Perhaps it was that flag which attracted one to cross the road — for its message speaks across the borders of nationalities and knows no boundaries or frontiers — and to come to the chaplain's car. In spite of the dust and grime of battle that still clung to him, the erstwhile foe looked less the part of a vanquished soldier than he did the plain simple man. *"Sprechen Sie Deutsch?"* — there was a hopeful gleam in his eye, which sparkled to a flame when he discovered that the chaplain could falteringly converse with him in his own tongue. He had recognized the flag — and because he loved the Saviour he had stopped to speak to the first Christian chaplain he had seen for a long time. One thing he wanted before he went back to the road to join the long column of his countrymen trudging on to the prison enclosures: to ask the Americans to preach Christ to the men they were taking captive, to ask if there would be chaplains in the prison camps. "We must have God with us when someday we go back to the fatherland, and you Americans must show him to us again, for we have lost him."

What will he find, as for a time he sojourns in America, waiting for the war to end and to be returned to his own land? Will he be able to say, "And God was there"?

Tomorrow

I

THE STRAIN of battle is over. For a time at least turmoil has been left behind as the division moves to rest in a bivouac far distant from the scenes of conflict. True, there is constant daily drill and training. Other campaigns are yet ahead, but for a while men will rest, and tired bodies and weary minds will be refreshed. Men must still sleep on the ground, but now straw is available to mattress the bumps and soften the hardness of earth, and the ingenious will find scraps of lumber to make themselves rude cots. The blackout is now only a nightly dimout, for the danger of enemy air attack is now many miles away. Long, hard hours of work in the hot African sun are still the soldier's lot, but when the day's work is done, there are trips to town — with its strange mixtures of native Arab quarters and colonials from the continent of Europe. The enchantment of Morocco creeps into a man's spirit — its walled cities remind him of ages past, and of other wars that have been fought. Its lazy, indolent customs bewitch him — they are all so different, and so interesting. But deep within him the

71

smoldering loneliness of long absence from home and loved ones burns with an ever-increasing heartache. It has been months since many of these men left the homeland; there will be many months more of anguish and pain and loneliness before they return. But now, for a time, the division is resting, while old men are preparing for further tasks and new men, come to take the place of those who would not again be with us, are taught what the old men had learned.

What does a man learn in months of battle? Who can fathom a man's heart and soul and mind? They had learned that men could face hour after hour and day after day of terror, and still go on. They had learned that after a while men pass the stage of weariness and fatigue — and still go on. They had learned the science of warfare. They had learned that life can be very cheap. They had learned how to fight, and how to keep on fighting. They had learned how to be wary, and how best to protect themselves. They had learned how to kill, and how to die — and how to live.

And some there were who had learned to know God. What would they now do with their knowledge? Now that the dangers were so far away, now that there were no foxholes or slit-trenches to crouch in while the bombs fell and the shrapnel scattered, now that there was so little to fear, what would be their reaction? If ever the true measure of a man would be discovered, it would be now, when tension and danger were passed and when body and soul and mind relaxed.

Honesty compels us to record that there were those who found relief in the easy moral laxity of foreign environment. Liquor, so long unavailable during many months of campaigning, now sparkled with its promised enchantment. Ladies — and too often those who were not ladies — offered companionship to lonely men who had seen only other men for long months. Temptation is ever ready for those who are willing to be tempted — and some after months of strain are all too willing. Even the cynic will admit that in society there are those to whom personal purity and righteousness mean little, but the cynic is not concerned about them: he wants to know about those who claim to be living on a higher level. He wants to know about men who under strain of battle and danger professed to a new idealism, claimed to have found God. He wants to know how such men act now when the dangers which brought them face to face with God are passed.

The chaplain, more than anyone else, perhaps, realized that this was now the time of real testing of men. Would that boy who " up there " that evening before he was to go on a raiding party at dawn had come to talk and pray with the chaplain — would that boy remember now the soul-searching confessions he had made that night? Would he still remember what he had said when after the raid had been successful he had come again to the chaplain: " He didn't let me down, sir, and I'll never forget my promise to him that I made last night."

And what about that sergeant who had been

wounded, and who said to the chaplain who kneeled beside the stretcher at the aid station: " Chaplain, I'm hurt bad. I can't die yet, — I never played fair with God. I've got to have another chance. Pray for me." What about that sergeant, now that he had finally recovered from his wounds and had rejoined the unit here at the rest camp? What would he do now that he had his other chance?

Or that other lad, who sat so long under the olive tree in the grove where so many bombs had fallen that day. What about him? He had said something that night about praying in his slit-trench, — praying so hard all that long day because he was afraid God would not listen to him. How could he expect God to listen to him when for so long he had paid no attention to God, when for so long he had deliberately sinned against his Saviour? That lad who, as the night wore on, discovered that God would always listen to a man — would he remember now that he had found the meaning of a Saviour's love and presence as under that olive tree before the new day dawned he had made his confession and pledged himself to the Master's way of living?

The chaplain remembered that officer who had lingered behind, following the little service held after dark in a deep wadi. " Chaplain, these men look to me for leadership. It's all very well to lead them into action — to give them their orders, to let them know that I am with them in it all — but that's not enough. I can't forget that in spite of all I do for them now,

I never set them a very decent example when we were back in Ireland and England." The chaplain remembered how often after that this officer and he had talked about these things. He remembered the Good Friday service when that officer had been among the little group of men who knelt to be baptized. The men who had been there that evening would remember that. What would they see now in that officer who had failed to set an example to his men before Africa — who now was a confessed Christian because of Africa?

Again honesty compels us to admit that there were some who in the strain had called upon the Lord, and prayed unto him whom they felt they needed, but who promptly forgot when the danger had passed. There have always been those who like the lepers of old sought the Master when they felt need for what he could give them, only to go their own way again when they had received of his love. But one there was who returned to give thanks, and it was to him the Saviour said, " Thy faith hath made thee whole."

There is no way to note the individual record of all those to whom the presence of God had become a reality as the months had passed, no way to chart the subsequent rise or fall of their new-found faith. But out of the maelstrom of battle this one truth became evident to him who as chaplain was concerned with the souls of men: when once a man has truly found God, that man never again loses sight of him; that man is a changed man. And some there were who had truly found him.

In the days of readjustment that the rest period offered, when men were forgetting the strain of past battles the while they prepared for coming engagements, the chaplain had many opportunities to follow the reactions of those with whom he had shared so much. His own faith, of which he had been so sure when many months ago he had volunteered to leave the security of a civilian parish, had grown deeper and richer and more full of meaning than ever it had been before — because you cannot help men to discover God without finding him anew yourself. And now, as day after day he observed men whose hearts had been laid bare before him, as he recalled how so many of them had promised their Saviour on bended knee to be true to him — now he saw fully the working of the Holy Spirit. They were not in the majority, these men of changed lives. Men living true Christian lives have never been in the majority. But who can tell how great the grain of mustard seed will grow? The testimony of the rest period was proof that for some God was there, as he had been there when they had found him in their loneliness and fear on the battlefield, as they had found him in places where men would not have thought to look for him. And the manner of their lives these days told that these men had not lost him. It is to bear witness to this that the chaplain who was there, and who saw, has tried to put into enduring form this story of men who found God; to share with others, who may still be searching, the discovery of the power of the presence of God in a man's life, and what that Presence can do in men's lives. " We cannot but speak the things which we have seen and heard."

II

There is yet another chapter that must be added to the story of men who have gone forth to war — another picture that is part of the account — unpleasant, heart-rending, and challenging. It is a chapter whose scenes follow long after the period of training, soon after the experiences of combat. This chapter deals with broken bodies, weary minds — and with men facing the future with a great question mark looming up before them. It is the picture of a great base hospital far behind the lines, to which are evacuated the more seriously wounded. To such a hospital men whose bodies and minds can no longer stand the strain of battle are sent from the smaller field hospitals. After a time in such a hospital, some may find anew the strength which sends them back to battle; others will go out to limited fields of service; but many will take the long voyage home — there to face months of further hospitalization before their broken bodies are whole again. Some will never be whole again — for war leaves scars no surgeon can ever cure, and war leaves minds that will never find rest again. At the crossroads between the hasty turmoil of war and the long tedium of readjustment stands the base hospital.

In the period of reorganization that followed the

campaign, the chaplain had to decide whether he should go on with the battalion or accept appointment to the staff of chaplains in such a hospital. Where could he render the most service? Where was the greatest need? To whom could he, personally, be of greater help — to men facing further battles or to men facing the great future with lives and minds that needed vast readjustments?

That he decided aright in accepting the appointment to the hospital staff, the chaplain soon realized. Going daily through the great wards, stopping beside this bed to speak a word, lingering with this group to share a story, doing an errand for this lad, speaking a word of encouragement, writing a letter, offering a prayer — so many little things, yet all important to those who were sick and wounded, as the chaplain could understand, because he too had been in battle — so many little things showed the chaplain the great need of these men. But back of it all lay the great problem, so often unexpressed: What is going to happen to me when I get home? Will I be able to hold a job? Will I be a care to loved ones? Will the scars heal, or will I have to face people who feel sorry for me whenever they look at me? What is going to happen to me?

To so many of these men the great postwar problem begins now — and to them it is a very personal problem. There is the lad who will never see again. As he gropes his way along, the physical darkness is still shattered by the blinding flash of the exploding shell, but there is no light in the darkness that looms ahead. Already he has learned that the darkness of uncertainty is denser than the deepest blackout through which he ever groped his way up front. No flares shoot skyward to show him the way out of the darkness now.

Over on yonder bed, is that a man encased in the great armor of plaster casts? Someday his body will be whole again — medical skill promises that. But during the long weeks he has already lain in his casts, during the long months still ahead before they will have all been removed, fearful questions perplex him. He is a farmer, and there is no one else to take over the farm when he returns and his aged father no longer can work. The farm must support his parents, and the wife and child he left waiting there, and himself, but he will never be strong enough to work a farm again. When the plane crashed that day, falling so fast before he could free himself from his tail-gunner's perch, the strength went forever from the strong farmer's body. Broken bones may knit again — but when too many have been crushed and broken, more than physical strength is gone.

The young lieutenant over yonder, taken from college before he graduated and placed in command of a platoon of tanks, leaving behind as he sailed from America " the prettiest girl in the world ": " And she promised to marry me as soon as I get home. Look at me now, Chaplain; I don't want her even to see me again " — as you looked at him on his bed, swathed from head to feet in great layers of salve-soaked bandages, you saw again a tank burning on the desert, and a young lieutenant thinking only of his men trapped in that tank, and you understood, for burns leave ugly scars, even when they cover a hero's body. But it is not a hero who thinks of " the prettiest girl in the world " — it is a lover whose broken heart is crying out, because he fears what he will look like to that girl when the bandages have been removed, because he loves her too dearly to face a sympathy he fears more than life itself!

And this fair-haired boy with his bandaged hand resting on his bandaged chest — you look twice before you realize that there is only one hand, only one arm lying across that wounded chest. He had been a skilled artisan, and the intricate work of the past was a mocking memory, for how could a skilled artisan go back to the work he loved without the skilled right hand to do that work — the only work he had ever known — the work that had been his dream since as a child he had learned its intricacies from a skilled father who in turn had learned it from his father.

Tragic pictures — all of them — for broken bodies, even though they may be skillfully repaired in part, mean heartache and anguish to those who must learn to live anew! Nor are broken bodies the only tragic pictures. Psychiatrists say that there is a limit to which every man's mind can stand the strain. Fortunately, for most men, that limit may be very far off. But there are many who, whenever they hear an airplane again, will involuntarily listen, hearkening if by chance it may be a dread dive bomber. There are many who in their minds will shudder at memories of sights and sounds that come back again to plague them. Yet these will be the men for whom the possible breaking point may be very far off. But there are others whose minds could not stand the strain. There is no sadder ward than that where men grope in their dark bewilderment, trying to find something that they have lost, trying to understand, trying to co-ordinate mind and thought and will. The horrors of war take a terrible toll. Where is the light in the darkness?

These may be the "serious cases" — these wounded, broken bodies, these perplexed minds. But the tragedy is that there are many such "serious cases" — men who left home and jobs to go to war, and who now must go home asking fearfully, "To what?" How will America receive them? Have we an answer for them — for these men who in the full strength of their youth went out from our land to fight that it might still be the land we want it to be? It is easy to phrase words of reassurance, to tell men of a Saviour who has promised, "In the world ye shall have tribulation: but be of good cheer; I have overcome the world." But men are going to need more than reassuring words. Many of these men have discovered in the turmoil of past months a new understanding of life and of God. The crucial test of new-found faith is yet to come in the months of rehabilitation, as broken bodies and lives adapt themselves to new conditions. The challenge is to the Christian Church.

How will it measure up, how will it atone for the failures of the past — failures that must be admitted, for had it not somehow failed, there would have been no war of man against man. It is this challenge that America must face — not only now as her wounded heroes come home, but tomorrow, and tomorrow, as the war finally ends, and men come home to live in the peace for which they fought and suffered, and for which so many died.

III

This has been a story of men who have found God. It has been a story of many men, but there are others of whom it has not told, for there are many who still are groping, who have yet to find him. It has been a personal story — but personal only that all who read it may be challenged by the message it brings.

There are other stories still untold, for the diary of a chaplain, were it not too sacred to share, would tell of many things. It would tell of men kneeling before their comrades as they confessed their faith in God. It would tell of prayer with dying men who, like the thief on the cross, turned at last to the Saviour. It would tell of the secrets of hearts poured out in conference and confidence to the chaplain, of intimate family problems, of heartache and loneliness, and of worry and fear. It would tell of letters written by the chaplain to mothers and fathers, and wives, and sweethearts; and of letters received by the chaplain as loved ones at home in their sorrow and heartache write to him on behalf of their boys so far away from them, but so near to the chaplain.

Would that these tender, beautiful stories were all that the diary would reveal! But there are other stories — unlovely, sordid, tragic tales. Armies are made up of all kinds of men. And were the diary to be opened too wide, it would tell of men who held no high principles, who never had eyes to see God. It would tell of men who drank too much, and of lives ruined by drunkenness. It would tell of men whose characters were ruined, and who soiled the characters of others. It would tell of remorse, and tragedy, and of men who sought the chaplain only because trouble made it expedient to do so. It would tell of letters written by the chaplain, trying to straighten out muddled affairs of sinful lives; and of pathetic letters received by the chaplain from those whose problems were the tragic results of sinfulness. That there were so many who did find God, and whose lives took on new meaning, makes the need of others the more noticeable — and gives us who think ourselves Christians cause to reflect, and to face the days ahead with new resolution. The challenge is to us, who in these days ahead must fit our returning men into the pattern of a new life.

We do not like to think of the Church as having failed. Gloriously we repeat again the Master's words, " I will build my church; and the gates of hell shall not prevail against it." We know that the Church of

83

Christ cannot fail. But men and women who make up that Church can fail Him who is its Head — and in failing him cause the work and influence of his Church to be greatly straitened. Perhaps in the maelstrom of today we are too near to conditions properly to analyze or understand the failures that allowed another war to come between the nations of the world. Great economic and political issues underlie the world's problems. But deeper still lies hidden the fact that Christ Jesus has given the world a way of love and brotherhood. Somewhere in the babble of sounds the still small voice has not been heard. Military strategists and political leaders will discuss ways and means of ending the war and of establishing the peace. The still small voice must be heard above the storm. It will be heard only as those who believe give sound to it.

If one word can characterize the mental state of the average person today, it is " confusion " — a blind groping after solid reality. Nowhere is this more clearly seen than in the minds of the men in our Army. To him who as chaplain has the privileged task of being the confidant of the men, their perplexing problems become a great concern. What a dark picture we have given them! We have preached a Christ who loves and is concerned about man, and life has given them a philosophy of totalitarianism, and said in effect, " Man is but a cog in a wheel." This is not the truth for which Christ died that man might live! This is not the truth which proclaims that there is nothing so vitally important in all this world as a human soul! Wherein has the Church failed these past years, that mankind should have lost the power of the vision of a Prince of Peace? Wherein must the Church succeed if it is to wield the power and the influence that are divinely its own in the postwar world?

Time after time the chaplain tried to answer this question in his own mind. In his civilian parish he had measured the success of his Church by the size of his congregation, by the increase of budgets, by the growing roll of communicants, by the many varied activities of his Church program. And because his, like so many other Churches, measured up favorably in comparison to certain man-made goals, he had felt that the Church of Christ was successful. And then the war came — and men paid no heed to angels singing " peace on earth." The Church, somewhere, had failed to herald that message of peace. Where had it failed? How could it assert the power of its influence in correcting its failure of the past?

Perhaps the answer — at least the beginning of the answer — is to be found in what a sergeant told the chaplain one day. Chapel was over. The several hundred men who a few minutes before had filled the mess hall to overflowing had gone again to their duties. Most of these men would tell you, when you had gained their confidence, that they had not attended Church with any regularity — some of them not at all — while they were in civilian life. But for some reason over here — far from home — they came in ever-increasing numbers. What, then, was the difference?

Had the sergeant found the answer? "Back home I lost interest in the Church because it was always raising money and doing so many things that didn't make any difference to me. Chapel over here is just worship, and one feels he gets near to God. Unless the Churches back home forget these unnecessary things and just make people think about God, they won't hold us when we get back."

Often in the months that followed, the chaplain was to be privileged to share the discovery of the presence of God with men who had not known him before. And many times he was to realize that the great secret of worship was found not in temples made with hands, but wherever " one feels he gets near to God." Like a prophetic challenge the sergeant's words still sound in his ears: " Unless the Churches back home forget unnecessary things and just make people think about God, they won't hold us when we get back."

And the Church must hold these men who have found God. Others still will find him before they come home — find him often through those who have already learned of his presence. Others still will need to find him. Like the Greeks of old, men tomorrow will be coming to his disciples as they came yesterday, as they come today, saying to the man who professes to know, " Sir, we would see Jesus." In all the great challenge of reconstruction in the postwar world, as disrupted lives and broken bodies are rehabilitated, the one great task of the Church of Jesus Christ must be to " make people think about God." Peace conferences of militarists and statesmen must settle great international issues. Politicians and economists must solve tremendous financial problems. Men and women must adapt themselves to new social orders. And in the days that follow, men must know that there can be no foundation for their plans and aims and hopes except the great foundation that is laid in Christ Jesus, no power to carry them out except in his strength, no hope in them except in his presence.

Out yonder, when dangers faced them, men found God very real. In the slit-trench as bombs rained around them, in the foxhole as artillery shells burst over them, they felt their own helplessness and called upon God, to discover that he was there. But even as they prayed, they saw their comrades die beside them. Now, when dangers have passed and life is quietly normal again, what will happen to their new-found faith? Our problem is, not that men shall find faith on a battlefield, but that they shall not lose that faith which they have found. Our task will be to see that the little they have discovered — for in the sudden face of danger men discover so little — is nourished and strengthened until it shall grow into a strong, abiding trust in the God who is always present.

This, then, is the challenge that faces anew the Church of Jesus Christ: to make real the presence of God in men's lives. It is not a challenge that can be accepted around a conference table, nor by great mass movements. It is still the individual challenge that it has ever been since the lonely Man of Nazareth walked in company with other men, bringing them one by one into fellowship with himself. It is still the individual challenge that it has ever been since first a man brought another man to Jesus. When peace comes it will be the same individual challenge that it was when through the noise of battle a man heard the still small voice and discovered that God was near.

If the Church of Christ has failed in the years that have passed, it has been the failure of its members to make real the presence of God in their daily lives. We have built our stately temples to the worship of God, and endowed our choirs and our pulpits. We have organized our work and undertaken great programs. We have exulted in pulpit oratory and in the numerical strength of our laity and our growing budgets. But too often our worship has ended there.

Someday — not too far away — our boys will come back from the far-flung battlefields of this Second World War. They will return to the homes of which they have dreamed these long months, to the office, the shop, the farm. They will come back again to take up life where they left it when they answered the call to serve the nation in its crisis. In their dreams they expect to find things the same when they return as when they left, for they think of themselves as being still the same boys who went out from our homes.

But they will not be the same boys that we proudly waved away as we tried to hold back the tears. Since last they saw their homes they have seen a world. They have visited nations of which we know so little, and lived amongst people of strange customs. They have fellowshiped with men of other religions and other creeds, and observed their cultures, studied their lives, and judged their views. They have lived through lonely, tragic days, and seen horrors and experienced never-to-be-forgotten moments. They will come back to our homes, to our towns and to our farms, to our shops and offices, and they will bring to our smug little communities a cosmopolitan outlook such as we have never known before. They will not be the same boys who went out from our homes, and no amount of wishful thinking will make them so. And though they return to the things of which they dreamed while they were away, they will unconsciously expect those things to have kept pace with their own changing views.

Great adjustments will have to be faced by these men of ours when they come home. Having analyzed political attitudes from the vantage point of distance, they will dare to suggest changes. They will not hesitate to see that their voice is heard in coming political issues. They have witnessed economic structures in many phases, and now are determined that the future shall be more wisely planned. After having experienced life on varied levels, they have formed new opinions of the social order. They have come to grips with life — and death — and formed new estimates of the value thereof. They have heard religion preached, and seen its weakness and its strength among the peoples of the world.

They will be coming home, these boys of ours, content at first to take up life where they left it months ago. But natures once satisfied by the daily routine will soon grow restless again as the call of the world they have seen stirs in their memories. They will not be content to sink back into the ruts of the past. Although they will come back to give it all a chance — for deep in their hearts they want what they have left — they will be ready to reject what does not satisfy them. They will be coming home to our Churches with new attitudes in their feeling toward religion.

The Church of Jesus Christ, more than ever before in recent generations, will be on trial in the minds of men. Its message — the same yesterday, today, and forever, — needs no change. But these men who are coming home will be looking with new interest to see what that message is accomplishing in our land. With eyes opened in new understanding of world conditions, they will evaluate Christianity as they have seen it in comparison with other norms of life. They will be desirous of worshiping God — in thanksgiving for their return to their homes, in memory of comrades whom they left out yonder where the small white crosses rise row on row. But deep underneath they will be looking for more than a place to worship. They will be looking for a norm which can bring sense and reality to a cosmopolitan world, which can give that basis for peace and brotherhood that will prevent another war. They will be looking to the Church of Christ for the establishment of that which they seek, for deep in their hearts they know the Church professes to be the instrument of God for good upon this earth, and they know, whatever their stated belief, that it will take some power greater than man to bring peace and sanity out of the chaos of these past years.

The Church of Christ must not fail these boys of ours when they come home again. They must be able to hear from its pulpit the stirring story of God's love for all mankind; they must learn from its Sacraments the meaning of fellowship offered to man by the Saviour; they must share its program and its services, knowing that the Church of Christ can justify its existence only when these programs and services reach out into every community to touch the hearts and lives of all men. And they must be able to look to us — to us to whom they have come back from their varied experiences in the far-flung world — for proof of the reality of God. Until we who profess to believe the old, old story can tell it plainly to others, in words and by our daily examples, its full power cannot be known.

They will be coming back to us — looking to us for assurance and for strength to face the trying days ahead as they re-establish themselves in a normal routine of life. They will be asking nothing of us except the chance to live their own lives. But they will be expecting sympathetic understanding of their new, cosmopolitan views, and perhaps sometimes be a bit impatient if we do not appreciate their changed attitudes and feelings.

Though they may not expect anything of us, there are things we can give them. Chief among our gifts is a living, dynamic faith in God and the Way of the

Master. Out yonder some found him, while many others came near to finding him. We must not let them lose the vision. The greatest gift we can offer them in our loving gratitude is that sure foundation upon which they can build anew their world: *our* faith in Christ Jesus. The greatest assurance we can give them as they face again the routine of life is to present evidence by *our* lives that *we* live in the presence of God. The greatest joy we can share with them as they come again to our homes is to have them discover anew therein the faith of their fathers — to find that God who seemed near them in their trouble is here, in the peace of the homeland, even as he was out there when in turmoil they felt the need of his presence.

This is *our* challenge! There are men who will still find God only as they find him in *our* lives. There are men who came near to finding him once, to whom *we* must show him now. There are men who found him far from home, to whom *we* must show his presence abiding here. *We* must make his presence so evident in *our* daily lives, that men knowing *us,* may always be able to say, " And God is here."